Ten Days
to Die

CE

Gingras

The Oracle

Author:
C.E. Gingras

Copyright © September 10, 2012

Book Type:
Print and E-book

Editors:
Sharmini Gingras
Heather Thurston

Publication Date:
October 2012

Publisher:
CreateSpace

Number of Pages:
49

Creator: C.E. Gingras

Cover Photo By:
Mee-Lin Woon

Table of Contents

Chapter Summaries — Quick reference guide complete at end of each day. Try memorizing what you are dying to each day 45-46

Preface

I was inspired to write this book while working on a paper for a History and Literature class of Ancient Israel back in July of 2004. Professor Bill Temple, PhD always encouraged me to complete it as a devotional study book. Though being a typical student, I took my time. I just want to say thank you Dr. Temple for never giving up on me and the encouragement you always provided me with.

As for actually completing the project I will have to say that next time I hope I am a lot closer to being actually dead to all the suggested life changes. It is one thing to discuss the theological academics of dying to self and a completely new thing in actually doing it. My thanks to God the Father, God the Son, and God the Holy Spirit for actually forcing me to live out everything I wrote about.

My prayers for you is that He may take hold of your life as He did mine so that you may learn what it is to be dead to yourself yet alive for Jesus Christ. – Amen –

Introduction:

At a glance, the book of Nahum declares the coming doom to the city of Nineveh. Though with refined study, a beautiful picture is exposed of God and His attributes. In this study, it is my desire that you die to everything born of self so that you may climb in the mountains God has chosen for you.

As I have matured, my walk with God has beckoned me closer to Him. When I respond to this call and strive for that intimate relationship with Him, often I come up short. If I am honest with myself, God's path for me is clear! Have you ever walked into a closed door or a tree large enough to derail a train? So maybe you and I are not so different. The only thing that has blocked our path is our focus! It is for this reason that I have chosen to pursue this bible study, so that both you and I may rid ourselves the distance between life and God.

In order for us to accomplish this, we are going to have to be dedicated not only to studying the Word of God, but also meditating on the truths. He will be teaching us through our normal daily grind.

Author:

All we know about the author is revealed to us in vs. 1:1, which essentially gives us his name -*Nahum* and the town he is from -*Elkosh*. The name *Nahum* means "comfort" and is connected with the name Nehemiah - which defined is: "The Lord comforts" or "comfort of the Lord." *Elkosh* is only mentioned this one time in the Bible as well. It is quite possible the village of Elkosh was renamed Capernaum, which in Hebrew translates – village of Nahum, but whether renaming actually happened is not known and remains a mystery.

Date:

In vs. 3:8, we are given reference to the fall of Thebes which was destroyed by the Assyrians in 663 B.C. So we know the book of Nahum was written sometime after 663 B.C. and sometime before 612 B.C. when Nineveh was destroyed.

Background:

Nahum was written approximately 150 years after Jonah prophesied to Nineveh, the capital of Assyria. After Jonah's prophecy, Nineveh repented and God spared their destruction. God also used the Assyrian empire to bring about His justice on the northern kingdom of Israel (Samaria) who had failed to keep her covenant obligations. In 722 B.C. the Assyrians captured Samaria and deported the Israelites. However, after that time the ways of the Assyrians became so intolerable that God chose to destroy them.

Getting Started:

Okay now that we have a brief introduction as to the bigger picture of what was taking place when Nahum wrote this book. Let's take a look at the context of God's Word in Nahum and what it can do to loosen the chains that keep us from helping ourselves! We will be using this Old Testament Oracle to enable you to do what the great theologian from the early Christian Church Paul did when he wrote in a letter to Galatia saying,

> "I have been crucified with Christ and I no longer live, but Christ lives in me. The life I live in the body, I live by faith in the Son of God, who loved me and gave himself for me. I do not set aside the grace of God, for if righteousness could be gained through the law, Christ died for nothing." Galatians 2:20, 21

That's right. This is what you and I will be working towards being able to say:

> "I have been crucified with Christ and I no longer live, but Christ lives in me."

Every day is going to be different in this journey, and I will help guide you into learning new aspects of God's grace.

With the title being "Ten Days to Die" I am not implying that I want you to achieve this goal in ten consecutive days. My intentions were for you to do this in two weeks. Stick with the study for 5 days and then take the week ends off and rest with a normal daily devotional that is relaxing and uplifting.

Remember if you are doing this in a small study group make sure and swap out names and phones numbers so you can contact each other for support; or to answer any questions that may arise.

Name:_____

Contact #:_____

Name:_____

Contact #:_____

Name:_____

Contact #:_____

Name:_____

Contact #:_____

Name:_____

Contact #:_____

Day 1

As we begin each day we are going to start out with a short prayer.

Dear Lord,

I thank You for this time we have together. As I study your Word today I ask that you teach me Lord, and make me aware of new truths so that I may come to know You in a more intimate way. – Amen -

By this point you have probably had many opportunities to ponder the thoughts about what it means to die in ten days. For your relief, there is no given formula. For one it may mean to die to lust or all forms of adultery. To another it means to die to greed or control, and yet others it maybe gossip or all of the above. Maybe you lie somewhere in between or in quite another place altogether. *Sin has many faces.* Whatever the case may be for you it is okay, because this is your journey to dying to that which binds you. You hold the reigns that are your guide.

So each day when you begin this study, I am going to be asking you to focus your thoughts in three areas. First, what is God trying to communicate to the people in this book? Secondly, what issues are similar or the same in your present life/world? And finally, how do you apply these Truths (Jn. 14:6 - Jesus Christ) to your life?

Today we are going to start out by reading Nahum 1:1-6. This will be the focus of our study, though if you have the time you may find it beneficial to read the entire first chapter. As a reminder, just remember while reading you are looking to see the bigger picture as it is spelled out in the fine detail of God's word.

I have never heard of a spiritual marathon before but I think this may be its equivalent.   Most devotional studies are set up for 30 days. We are going to accomplish what they do and more in just 10 days. It shouldn't take any extra time each day. We are just going to cut a little deeper. No worries, you may find that it is a walk in the park. Go ahead and read Nahum 1:1-6 now.

From the start, we are informed this book is an "oracle." In this case the use of the word "oracle" is to mean a divine prophecy associated to a burden. Simply stated it is a divine message of doom. Unlike the book of Jonah, Nahum did not preach this message in the streets of Nineveh. It was delivered in book form to Nineveh according to vs. 1.   It is unclear why such a message had to be revealed in the form of a book. Maybe Nahum was not well, or maybe the message was not only meant for those of Nineveh?

Who do you think a message like this would help?_____
_____
_____

Or why do you think it was written verses being oral – food for thought?_____
_____
_____

Following this in verse 2, God reveals His wrath and power. But, before we get caught up in His awesome power, what word in this vs. keys us into why God is angry?_____

That is right. God is jealous. Have you ever been jealous with a family member or friend for how they treated you after you gave them everything? You offered part of yourself – compassion, love, labor, or a pricey piece of your heart only to have it forced back upon you? Well that is what Nineveh has done to our Lord. When Jonah brought Nineveh the message of the Lord to *repent or be destroyed*, they repented. When God saw this, he had compassion on them and did not destroy them as planned (Jonah 3). God forgave them and fully restored them only to have them reject Him again and again in the future.

Have you ever witnessed this perverse behavior in your life? What does that look like with family, friends, school mates, and work colleagues?_____
_____
_____

Read verse 3 again.

Lucky for us the Lord is slow to anger. It is in His nature to give us time to make things right before Him. *Is there any area in your life that you would like to die to right now?* If so take a moment and be real with God. Talk to Him about the hold it has on you. Ask for His hand in help. Grieve in the loss of its worldly security it provided you and the separation it put between you and your Lord, God, and Savior. According to James it says,

"Submit yourselves, then to God. Resist the devil, and he will flee from you. *Come near to God and he will come near to you...*". James 4:7-8

If there is someone you need to ask forgiveness from, or someone you need to hold yourself accountable to your submission write their name(s) down now so you can humbly present yourself before them for forgiveness and/or guidance.__
_____
_____
_____
_____
_____

Now let's take a look at *El Shaddai* - God's awesome power (vs. 3-6). God's illustration of His power shows how ill equipped Nineveh was to stand against Him. However this is not only a message of doom to Nineveh. It is also a message of triumph to the tribe of Judah who were being threatened by their Assyrian neighbors. We have access to amazing power beyond our comprehension! Aren't you glad to have a Father like that on your side? What powers of this world can stand against Him?

When God is about to do something big He often reveals His plans in advance. What has God been trying to reveal to you? _

_____
_____
_____

What are you going to do about God's revelation?_____
_____
_____
_____

Today I want you to **die to the control you think you have on your life.** Remember to keep Abba Father (Abba = Daddy) close. If you have a question, ask Him. Then quietly listen for His voice. You will know it is Him when He speaks.

Who are you going to share this with today?_____
_____

To give you an idea about not having control on your life, at one time I was using the internet to try to date. This was before most dating services and social networks. I was in a chat room with a cheesy name 'agirlsdream'. One day when I did not expect it I got a sarcastic response messaged back to me asking, "So whose dream do you think you are?" My reply "Yours of course." "Her response was 'LOL' (LOL=laugh out loud)." We bantered a little more and she finally asked, "What are you doing online in this chat room anyway?" I replied, "Looking for a wife, Isn't it obvious?" Her response was, "Good luck!" Shortly after this we both realized we lived on opposite sides of the world. So there was no pressure flirting and it was just fun and jokes until our cheeks hurt. As time passed the pain increased and it was our Lord who soothed our ailments.

Have you ever wondered who holds the Lord's hand when He is missing you?_____

_____

_____

_____

_____

_____

_____

_____

Later you will learn more about how little control we have on our lives! Especially with my story above, I experienced how little control I had and have over my life (and how God has a master plan for all of us).

Day 2

Father,

May you honor the time I am giving you today and bless me with eyes that see beyond structure, a heart and soul that thirst for the righteousness that You desire me to learn today.

– Amen –

Before we begin, let's go back a day and brief what you learned yesterday.

What are the three areas from day one you need to focus on each day?

1. _____
   _____

2. _____
   _____

3. _____
   _____

In today's lesson, we will be focusing on verses 7 and 8 in the 1st chapter of Nahum. Please prayerfully read through those verses a couple of times at this point.

Right off in verse 7, we are given an insight to the Lord's nature; that He is good. As you think back to your own experiences, can you remember a time when you received the goodness of the Lord? Go ahead and write a summary of what that experience was like._____
_____
_____

_____
_____
_____
_____
_____
_____
_____
_____
_____
_____

Next we learn about His protection in days of trials. You may have a personal experience of this too. It is comforting to know that He will protect those He cares for and trust in Him, as the latter part of verse 7 states.

In Nahum's letter, who do you think vs. 7 was written for?_____
_____
_____
_____
_____

That is correct. It was written for the tribe of Judah's benefit. But it is every bit as applicable for us today as it was for the tribe of Judah then.

> "The Lord is a good refuge in times of trouble." "He cares for those who trust in him but with an overwhelming flood he will make an end of Nineveh; He will pursue his foes into darkness." Nahum 1:7

What implication does that passage have for you? Have you ever forgotten to die to your own desires when the troubles of your world seem to overwhelm you? This passage reminds us to trust in God during time of trials. If you are to lose everything and are forced to live under laws in a land that is not your own, God can deliver you and even bless you with more. Just look at what He did for His servant Job. What's more important is that you remember during difficult times that your life belongs to God for His use and His pleasure and to fulfill the purposes He has chosen for you before creation began.

What burdens in your life are you struggling with today?_____
_____
_____
_____
_____
_____
_____
_____

   Take a moment and set fire to the torment these burdens have caused you. Then with whatever is left that needs to be dealt with, sit down with Jesus and ask Him to bring you help, send you guidance, and finally deliver you!

   Verse 8 is exciting because we see the deliverance of the Lord to Judah from the Ninevites in the following manner: "with an overflowing flood He will make a complete end" of His adversaries. The meaning of floodwaters was twofold in this instance. First off, it meant literally that a flood would overcome Nineveh. Additionally, floodwaters symbolized a powerful invading arm. Historians tell us the Medes and Babylonians invaded Nineveh with a combined force of four hundred thousand men. Isn't it good to know that God's deliverance is complete? Humanly speaking it appears God used more force than was necessary, but from God's perspective that was not the case.

Have you ever heard God's voice so loud and clear in your own life? If so what was (is) He saying to you?_____

_____

_____

_____

_____

_____

_____

To give you an example of this, thinking back to my earlier story where we don't always have control in our lives, that woman I met on-line that we started out with jokes ended up as my wife. She was living in Malaysia, her home country, at the time. I was in the United States. Because of the distance, we didn't think anything would happen and were more open and honest than if we'd been face to face. After several months of chatting with her on the internet, God provided a way for me to visit her. Again God showed us we were not in control of our destiny. Prior to leaving, I was 95% sure I would propose to her shortly after my arrival. I did do it within the first week of being there. God also provided a way for me to move out there and we were married approximately 12 months after my arrival. The truly amazing fact is that God had been speaking to her and preparing her heart approximately 15 months before we even met on the internet. He had told her that she would be leaving Malaysia to live in a foreign country sometime in the near future. This message God bestowed upon her heart came to pass 37-38 months after He revealed it to her. We moved to the United States approximately six months after our marriage. Had God not begun preparing her years in advance, this difficult move for her would have seemed impossible.

I share this example with you in an attempt that you not lose sight of the words God has spoken to your heart. Often God's revelation begins a journey and does not come to pass until He has had a chance to work out all the details in your life. He also works with all the other individuals He will be using to bring fulfillment of His revelation. For instance, when my wife received the message that she would be leaving Malaysia, I was nowhere near ready for a relationship of marriage caliber, nor willing to move to the other side of the world. When God did call me to go, I had to die to many dreams I had of living here in the U.S., just like my wife had to die to her comfortable way of life living in her home country.

Don't give up. Remember it is a journey. What is it in your own life you can change today that will bring you a step nearer to where God can fulfill His promises?_____

_____

_____

Looking back to the latter part of verse 8, we read that God "will pursue His enemies into darkness." This is quite a contrast to the light Nineveh was given when God sent His message through Jonah. If we reject the light long enough; God will deliver us into our hearts desires. Be careful that you do not partake or entertain thoughts in the ways of the world.

As we conclude today's lesson take a moment to reflect on what God has been teaching you.

Looking back to the first question in today's study about God's goodness, what message was God revealing to you behind the gift?_____

_____

_____

Today I want you to **die to the picture perfect life you have always dreamt of**. Life is hard, difficult and challenging. God is going to use those challenges to shape your character in such a way that He will be able to use you beyond your wildest dreams. *So let Him.*

Look for an opportunity to share the goodness of God with someone today!

Day 3

Heavenly Father,

We pray for strength today against all the unforeseen trials that will cross our paths. May you plant our feet in springs of heavenly water so we may be deeply rooted and not fall. – Amen –

The perfect life exists but just not in our own preconceived notion of it. Often we are at war between what we believe our life ought to be like and the direction God has called us.

Let's take a look at our text for today (Nahum 1:9-13) as we ask the Lord to guide us through it.

Right off in verses 9-11, I can see lots of trouble. Nineveh has chosen a difficult life that is in opposition to the life God desires them to live in. In verse 11 Nineveh is labeled, "One who plots evil against the Lord and counsels wickedness."

This sounds pretty serious, but it also makes me stop and think in what areas have I plotted against the Lord? I don't think of myself as evil or a counselor of wickedness, yet I know I have crossed those lines many times in thoughts if not in actual deeds. One of Jesus' closest disciples Peter in the New Testament is rebuked by our Lord Jesus after stating he would never let the elders in Jerusalem make Jesus suffer many things, and then kill Him. In which,

"Jesus turned and said to Peter, 'Get behind me Satan! You are a stumbling block to me; you do not have in mind the things of God, but the things of men'" Matthew 16:21-23.

This passage has opened my eyes to the workings of evil. There is the downright plotting of evil like the leaders of Nineveh and the elders, chief priests, and rulers of the law in the New Testament planned. Then there is the evil Peter fell into. In Peter's case his intentions seemed good but they were not in line with the plan God had called His Son Jesus Christ to.

Reflect on your own life for a moment. What are some examples where you have fallen into evil while having the best intentions of being obedient to the plans God has called you to?

_____
_____
_____
_____
_____

Probably the most common area we as Christians fall into (that is similar to Peter) is being an enabler to those whom we are close to like family and friends. Everyone has their hiccups. And sometimes when our friend with the hiccup is in the midst of a trial and we try to help them out, we don't. Often we do not speak the truth for fear of hurting their feelings. Then only later we find our efforts were misinterpreted and the help we gave allowed them further access to their thorn.

In regards to sin where has God called you to stand?_____
_____

That is right. We are to stand apart from it.

How are you to stand apart from sin?_____
_____

Strong and proud is a good starting point.

What are you going to do if sin blows your way or pulls and clings to your clothing?_____
_____
_____

Run with all your might in the opposite direction, and keep your hope in the Lord.

> "Even youths grow tired and weary, and young men stumble and fall; but those who hope in the Lord will renew their strength. They will soar on wings like eagles; they will run and not grow weary, they will walk and not be faint." Isaiah 40:30-31

This would be a good point to forget about the rest of our passage today, but we still need to address this last issue of Judah. The Lord broke their yoke from the neck of Assyria, tearing away their shackles (verse 13). What a blessing for Judah to be free again. Remember that they had failed to keep their covenant obligations. Essentially they were being disciplined under Assyrian rule until they were ready to turn back to their Heavenly Father.

God Disciplines His Children

> "My son do not make light of the Lord's discipline, and do not lose heart when he rebukes you, because the Lord disciplines those he loves, and he punishes everyone he accepts as a son." Heb. 12:5-6

- Judah trusted in the Lord and therefore was disciplined and released.
- Nineveh stopped trusting in the Lord some 150 years after Jonah preached repentance in the streets, and then God pursued them into darkness.

Today I want you to *die to a life of self-indulgence*. A little of a good thing is healthy, but too much will change from good to evil. This is true especiallywhen it separates you from God, and changes your morals and values. Then you may refuse to return to a righteous life like Nineveh did. In Peter's case, he was so caught up on keeping Christ to himself that he lost sight to the fact that we and the rest of the world would need Him too.

Day 4

Lord,

Help me to block out all the background noise in my life, so that I can be refreshed by Your voice Lord, and Your voice alone thus enabling me to walk and live in Your strength.
– Amen –

We have reached the fourth day, and are almost halfway through the Ten Days of Death. I hope and pray the journey thus far has been freeing and has given you a new perspective on the life God has called you to.

As a quick refresher so far we have died to:

Day 1   The control you think you have on your life.

Day 2   The picture perfect life you have always dreamt of.

Day 3   A life of self-indulgence.

Yesterday, we talked about the perils of the self-indulgent life. Today, we will learn about how effects of a self-centered godless life can harm society. However, we will also experience the contrast of a society returning to God, and the deliverance He provides for those who are ready to come home.

Today we are going to *die to your own plans of travel/vacation, and destination.*

Please Review Nahum 1:14-15 a couple of times.

In verse 14, the Lord is pretty specific about the upcoming destination for Nineveh saying,

"...I will prepare your grave for you are vile" declares the Lord. Nahum 1:14

Enough said for the self-centered godless life! However, verse 15 paints a totally different picture for the destiny of Judah, a society returning to God.

"Look, there on the mountains, the feet of one who brings good news, who proclaims peace! Celebrate your festivals, O Judah, and fulfill your vows. No more will the wicked invade you; they will be completely destroyed." Nahum 1:15

Their deliverance is foretold and what a beautiful picture it is.

Where is the one who brings good news and proclaims peace?
_____

What is Judah commanded to do?_____
_____

What promise are they given regarding the Assyrians their persecutors?_____
_____
_____

What is really exciting about this passage is that it not only speaks to Judah, but, it is a prophetic promise about the *good news* that will be preached to the world through Jesus Christ.

"The word is near you; it is in your mouth and in your heart that is the word of faith we are proclaiming: That if you confess with your mouth, 'Jesus is Lord,' and believe in your heart that God raised him from the dead, you will be saved." Rom. 10:8-9

"And how can they preach unless they are sent? As it is written, *How beautiful are the feet of those who bring good news!*" Rom. 10:15

You may be asking yourself what does this all have to do with dying to plans of travel/vacation, and destination? Let me explain. As God's word states in the book of Romans, if you confess your sins to Jesus and believe He was raised from the dead, *you will be saved.* Therefore we can stand, and stand proudly for we know no matter what happens, our salvation is sealed in place with Christ. So we do not place our confidence in the plans we make of where to go and what to do, because those plans can lead to disappointment. Rather we place our confidence in the path God provides for us.

Why don't you tell me about a time when you followed a path God provided for you?_____

_____
_____
_____
_____
_____
_____

Let me share with you a time my wife and I had to follow the path God had planned for us apart from our own path. We had been married about six months and were living in Malaysia where we got married. I had been having a difficult time finding full time work that would provide an income, so we were looking to relocate. After much thought, debate and prayer we decided to move to the United States. In order to make this move happen, there were a lot of hurdles we needed to jump.

When it came down to it the most time consuming piece was getting my wife's US permanent residency (PR) processed and established before departing from Malaysia. According to the US embassy, this process could be done in one month as long as we kept on top of things and submitted the required information in a timely and orderly fashion.

At the time my wife was teaching law courses at a private college, so we decided our departure date would be approximately one week after the end of her last class taught for the quarter. After arriving at that date, my wife gave her resignation notice one month in advance as required. I gave the owner of our apartment one month notice. We put my wife's car up for sale, contacted a shipping company and began selling our furniture.

As required for the PR visa, my wife had to receive every vaccination conceivable, get chest x-rays to rule out tuberculosis, have a complete physical and submit paperwork to the Malaysian government for a background check. The latter was the part that could take up to four weeks. The American Embassy was very helpful in making sure we were completing all the necessary steps. They were even kind enough to let us know right away when things had cleared on their end. Four weeks finally come around, and my wife and I had a week to make all the final arrangements.

However, we had no news from the Malaysian government on the status of the background check. All they would say was that it was in the process. By the end of following week, nothing had changed. I was able to convince my landlord to let us stay in the apartment for one more month but not any longer as he was eager to lease the place out for another year. I was told not to call the Malaysian government too often about the back ground check as that may upset them and give them an excuse to drag their feet.

The next two weeks went by very slowly with no news to report on the background check. Initially we were concerned about how we would hold out financially with my wife no longer having an income. Then it turned out that they had not filled her teaching position and had to hire her back at an hourly rate to teach the following term. That hourly rate just happened to be almost 3 times more than the normal contract rate so we were quite blessed.

As my wife went back to work, we set aside all the things we were bringing to the United States. The problem was that we could not tell the shipping company when to ship it or where to ship the container to in the US. God blessed us again here as the shipping manager was a British expatriate who sympathized with us and our situation. He agreed to hold our belongings locked up on the dock until we knew when we were leaving for the United States.

The little victories we experienced during this time brought us such joy that we cried before the Lord in thankfulness.

I continued to call the Malaysian government regarding my wife's background check and always got the same reply. At about four weeks, I started calling daily. I was informed my daily inquiries would not speed up the process. At which point I informed them that I had nothing left to do but call them. So the daily calls continued. It did not occur to me that I could be messing around with God's timing and I hope I did not upset Him by making those extra calls.

At about this time we had to leave the apartment we were living in. The rest of the furniture that we could not sell we gave away to family and friends and soon, we were homeless.

I can't quite remember how it came about if we asked or were offered a room at a friend's house but before long we were staying with missionaries and their kids from New Zealand. These missionaries and their kids had married us and made our marriage ceremony more than we could have ever dreamed it could be; and once again they were there to help in a stressful time when we were moving. This was another huge blessing! The love we experienced from this entire family will be passed down from generation to generation in our family.

It was about the 10th or 11th week when the background check finally arrived at the US Embassy and the rest of the paperwork was processed for her PR. The only thing left was getting rid of her car, and in the last couple of days prior to departure, a good friend (my best man from our wedding) decided to buy the car. We got our plane tickets and soon were off to the United States.

Now God could have allowed this whole procedure to go as smooth as possible. Do you think we would have learned anything about God and how He works if He had? To this day we use this experience as a baseline to guide us on how God works through our lives. It constantly reassures us to hold onto the faith of the important life changes God has foretold us about, regardless of the circumstances. Now I may have this passage backwards but when Matthew writes in his book chapter 14 vs. 25-30

> "During the fourth watch of the night Jesus went out to them, walking on the lake. When the disciples saw him walking on the lake, they were terrified. 'It's a ghost' they said, and cried out in fear. But Jesus immediately said to them: "Take Courage? It is I. Don't be afraid." "Lord, if it's you," Peter replied, "tell me to come to you on the water." "Come" he said. Then Peter got out of the boat walked on water and came toward Jesus. But when he saw the wind, he was afraid and, beginning to sink, cried out 'Lord save me'" Matthew 14:25-30

Often I feel like it is my family and I who are walking on water, but Christ is there with us holding our hands! We are so scared to lose eye contact or even look down to see if we are walking on water our focus and action singularly become the same. We just trust in faith that it will all hold together as long as we don't bat an eye ;).

Day 5

Dear God,

Deliver me into the presence of my Heavenly family today so that we may stand united and undefeatable, bringing glory to Your most precious Name. – Amen –

Just as a refresher what is one reason why we need to die to our preconceived plans of travel/vacation and destination?_____

_____
_____
_____
_____
_____
_____

Today's study is going to be covering Nahum 2:1-4. As Nahum's oracle regarding Nineveh has stated all along, Nineveh is destined for complete annihilation. Today we will begin to see how God plans to bring his vengeance out on Nineveh. Why don't you take a moment now, and read this passage a few times.

In verse 1, we learn the attackers are advancing on Nineveh. It also gives advice on some precautions they are to take. So Nineveh is under attack and yet they will not survive, but let's flip this around a bit.

What if you were under attack, what precautions would you have taken to survive?_____

_____
_____
_____
_____

The passage that speaks to me the loudest about preparation for battle, which also exposes God's eternal power, is titled *The Armor of God.* This passage is found in Ephesians 6:10-18, where the apostle Paul writes to encourage the early church of Ephesus. Paul says,

"Finally, be strong in the Lord and in His mighty power. Put on the full armor of God so that you can take your stand against the devil's schemes. For our struggle is not against flesh and blood, but against the rulers, against the authorities, against the powers of this dark world and against the spiritual forces of evil in the heavenly realms. Therefore put on the full armor of God, so that when the day of evil comes, you may be able to stand your ground, and after you have done everything, to stand. Stand firm then, with the belt of truth buckled around your waist, with the breastplate of righteousness in place, and with your feet fitted with the readiness that comes from the gospel of peace. In addition to all this, take up the shield of faith, with which you can extinguish all the flaming arrows of the evil one. Take the helmet of salvation and the sword of the Spirit, which is the word of God. And pray in the Spirit on all occasions with all kinds of prayers and requests. With this in mind, be alert and always keep on praying for all the saints."

ARE YOU PREPARED FOR BATTLE?

Have you ever felt captive or entrapped by the circumstances or the place God has allowed you to dwell in?_____

_____

_____

I am certain this is how the tribe of Judah felt just before the Lord restored them. Being held captive by the Assyrians was no pretty picture. But listen to what we learn of the Lord in verse 2,

"The Lord will restore the splendor of Jacob like the splendor of Israel, though destroyers have laid them waste and have ruined their vines."

'Restoring the splendor of Jacob like the splendor of Israel' is mind boggling and truly amazing. Jacob is the blessed son of Isaac who wrestles with God in Genesis it says,

"Then the man said, 'Your name will no longer be Jacob, but Israel, because you have struggled with God and with men and have overcome'". Genesis 32:28

Then we can learn something about his splendor in Genesis 35:11-13, which says,

"And God said to him, 'I am God almighty; be fruitful and increase in number. A nation and a community of nations will come from you and kings will come from your body. The land I gave to Abraham and Isaac I also give to you, and I will give this land to your descendants after you.' Then God went up from him at the place where He had talked with him." Genesis 35:11-13

So today *I want you to die to the idea of being held captive by life's circumstances.* There is nothing too big to get between you and where God wants you to be. In being where God wants you to be, you will truly understand His joy and peace.

Let me share with you a little childhood story that briefly held me captive by life's circumstances. It was one Sunday night and we had a special speaker. It was a speaker who needed a donation offering for support of his ministry. (I was maybe 11 or 12 years old but had a paper route and made more money than any other 11-12 year old around). That silver plate with the red velvet center got closer and closer and I could remember scripture saying, 'Give with one hand while the other hand does not know what it is doing.' To make things worse I was not only touched by the message and was eager to give for that reason, but there was also this brunette sitting next to me that I wanted to impress. She was already making my heart pound and stomach ache and it would not be right for me to give and show off in front of her. So when that silver plate got closer, I remember reaching into my right front pocket pulling out my wad of cash. First, I thumbed through the miscellaneous ones.Then I thumbed through a couple of fives and finally landed on my last 20. I took a big breath peeled it out of the roll and dropped it in the plate so little miss brunette could see. The fact that I was flaunting the Lord's gift around to appease my hormonal appetite may have sent me straight to hell if you had ever heard and believed the gospel the way my father taught it.

As it turned out there was a junior high retreat I was planning on attending that I needed to pay for myself. I no longer had enough money to go. Now what was I going to do? A couple days later I received a letter in the mail and it was not even my birthday! Readers Digest had sent me something and I was excited I would be the only 11-12 year old in town with a subscription to Readers Digest. Getting a subscription was not the request. But rather simply a check for $35 for winning a contest I had never entered. The Lord looked at my heart and saw it was genuine. I was not only able to go on the retreat but learned a valuable lesson that day which I will cling to when I feel forgotten.

Back to the attack, in verses 3-4 we get a vivid picture of what all the chaos is going to look like as Nineveh falls. The text itself is not really all that clear as to whom the soldiers and warriors are as it could either be the Assyrian war chariots running around confused or the invading attackers.

Day 6

Heavenly Father,

We know you are righteous in all You do, and will punish the wicked to the full extent of Your law for all they have done wrong. But today Lord, I pray You have mercy on one soul, and if you can spare one soul, why not two? Just lead me and give me your word of salvation that will transform their lives for all eternity. – Amen –

I know we have been through a lot together already and sometimes the initial death to part of your life is a lot easier than living it out. So let's just take a moment to see how you have done so far. I want you to name one item you have been able to die in the previous five days.

How have you died to the idea of being in control of your life? _
_____

How have you died to your idea of your picture perfect life?   _
_____

How have you died to a life of self-indulgence?_____
_____

How have you had to die to your plans of travel/vacation, and destination?_____
_____

How have you had to die to the idea of being held captive by life's circumstances?_____
_____

I know that it is tough to continue to die to these concepts each and every day. Just remember that it is not your strength you are to rely on. God sent us a King to do it for us. How awesome is that? In the book of Mark he quotes,

"If you can?" said Jesus. "Everything is possible for him who believes." Mark 9:23

Just believe it!

Let's get busy. It is time for battle. Are you ready? What is your house going to look like when your day comes?

Go ahead and read your text for today a few times through Nahum 2:5-10. Let me just briefly summarize this one for you. Everything that could possibly go wrong from a defensive point of view did go wrong. The city was flooded. The main palace collapsed. Commerce was completely stopped. Every cry of help went unheard. Every valuable item taken and all the people if still alive were stunned to the bone and pale.

Now given you are not in the city of Nineveh, but you may be in battle right now as you continue to die to new areas of yourself. Remember yesterday we read Ephesians 6:10-18 and talked about putting on the full armor of God. Have you put your armor on today? Maybe you need a little pick me up and should take a few minutes praying through assembling your armor. Just go back to yesterday's message and read Ephesian 6:10-18 on page 26.

Yesterdays and today's message coincide with each other to a certain extent. Yesterday you died to the idea of being held captive by life's circumstances. Today I want you to **die to the idea that there is never going to be a new day in your life.** You see in the midst of battle sometimes we lose our focus. If you keep your eyes on Jesus, you can have a thousand new days. The Psalmist says,

"This is the day the Lord has made; let us rejoice and be glad in it. O Lord, save us; O Lord, grant us success. Blessed is he who comes in the name of the Lord. From the house of the Lord we bless you. The Lord is God, and he has made his light shine upon us. With boughs in hand, join in the festal procession up to the horns of the altar. You are my God, and I will give You thanks; you are my God, and I will exalt You. Give thanks to the Lord, for He is good; His love endures forever." Psalms 118:24-29

Let us exalt in the Lord together, and watch as 'His love' blankets us.

Day 7

Dear Lord,

Help me to die to whatever material possessions I may feel I have earned a right to. For I know all blessings come from above and if there is something you want back from me help me to freely release it back to You. – Amen –

What is left after your battle? Since day one on this journey we have given, given, and given some more. So let me ask. Where are you today?_____

_____

I would think you should be somewhere between God and where you started. Take a moment to meditate and think about the pictures He has placed in your heart about what His plans are for your life right now.

What are His plans for your life right now?_____

_____
_____
_____
_____

Has the Lord revealed anything new to you about your life?_____

_____
_____
_____

His plans are perfect and amazing!

So what do you think it is time to do?

"As he looked up, Jesus saw the rich putting their gifts into the temple treasury. He also saw a poor widow put in two very small copper coins. 'I tell you the truth,' He said, 'this poor widow has put in more than all the others. All these people gave their gifts out of their wealth; but she out of her poverty put in all she had to live on.'" Luke 21:1-4.

You may wonder why the Father expects so much. It is because He wants to bless you,

"Give and it will be given to you. A good measure, pressed down, shaken together and running over, will be poured into your lap. For with the measure you use it will be given to you" Luke 6:38.

Have you ever given like the poor widow had done? Most of us haven't and there are only two reasons why. Either God has never required it from you, or you disobeyed when He did. The point I am getting at is taken from Matthew who says,

"...Freely you have received, freely give." Matt. 10:8

Stay close to God and then when He asks of you, in faith freely give.

Now let us look to today's scripture Nahum 2:11-13 and see how this all ties in together. The Assyrians were quite proud and powerful people who took life and captured cities at will, like a lion. The lion figure is a key element in their society. In nature, the lion is at the top of the food chain and has no natural enemies. The lion spoke volumes about who the Assyrians were and what they were about in their own eyes. They had no equals. *They were* the top of the food chain.

However, God mocks their feigned superiority. He destroys the lion, lioness and her cubs. The lions had nothing to fear until they met their maker and destroyer, The Lord God Almighty. There is not even a voice left and no messenger to report her destruction.

In the beginning of the study we talked about shedding some of our material wealth which is really irrelevant as it will not stand to pass the ebbing of time and we can't take it with us. However, when you take a closer look you find that you may possess titles and credits that you value more than your material possessions. You see the Assyrians were like kings. They were like lions in their own rights by definition of their rapacious ways. As you have read for yourself, God Almighty stripped them away from that entitlement.

So let me ask you. Are there any entitlements you are holding on to? If so, what are they?_____
_____
_____
_____

What really holds you? Is it the money in your pocket or the power behind your entitlement associated with your position in this life that defines who you are?_____
_____
_____

Jesus addresses the twelve disciples and who the greatest was when,

"They came to Capernaum. When he was in the house, He asked them, 'What were you arguing about on the road?' But they kept quiet because on the way they had argued about who was the greatest. Sitting down, Jesus called the Twelve and said, 'If anyone wants to be first, he must be the very last, and the servant of all.'" Mark 9:33-35.

Let's finish today by investing in that which lasts. You can start doing that *by dying to the security you hold in your social standings, employment status and entitlements.*

Day 8

Almighty God,

I realize this battle is yours Lord. May you never let me lose sight of that fact. If I pick up a sword to fight, may it be for you my Lord and You alone. – Amen –

Reflecting on yesterday, what titles has God asked you to rid yourself of so you may lie them down at His feet?_____

_____

_____

In the past few days, we have watched Nineveh collapse in comparison to her previous greatness. While at the same time you have been dying to the parts of your life that hold you captive; either fear or the position they entitle you to. Today we will begin to examine Nineveh from the position of her total destruction. So go ahead and take this time as an opportunity to read through your text (Nahum 3:1-7) a few times.

When you read verses 1-4 you get a picture of what Nineveh was like before her fall. It is not a pretty picture. Nineveh is known as the 'city of blood' because of how she massacred her rivals. The city gates were often marked off with pyramids of heads after a conquest. You may say that that was one of her calling cards. In verse 5-7, we see the Lord's response to her repulsive activities. The Lord is making an example of her so that others do not follow in her footsteps.

It is obvious why the Lord had to begin this battle. It is because of the atrocities Nineveh had committed. Evil had to be exposed so that the Lord could be revealed as triumphant.

> "The Lord will march out like a mighty man, like a warrior he will stir up his zeal; with a shout He will raise the battle cry and will triumph over his enemies."
> Isaiah 42:13

Now let's take this a step over to the more personal side. How is the Lord revealed as triumphant in your life?_____

_____

_____

_____

_____

_____

The apostle Paul writes to the Corinthians by saying,

> "But thanks be to God, who always leads us in *triumphal procession in Christ* and through us spreads everywhere the fragrance of the knowledge of Him. For we are to God the aroma of Christ among those who are being saved and those who are perishing. To the one we are the smell of death; to the other, the fragrance of life." 2 Corinthians 2:14-17

It was after the flood that

> "...Noah built an altar to the Lord and, taking some of all the clean animals and clean birds, he sacrificed burnt offerings on it. The Lord smelled the pleasing aroma and said in his heart: 'Never again will I curse the ground because of man, even though every inclination of his heart is evil from childhood. And never again will I destroy all living thing creatures as I have done'" Genesis 8:20-21.

I used these two passages to draw out the importance of the aroma that comes with the burnt offering. In the Old Testament Noah had to use clean animals a sacrifice, but in the New Testament it is the sacrifice that Christ paid on the cross that creates the aroma "in Christ and through us spreads everywhere the fragrance of the knowledge of Him." 2 Corinthians 2:14

According to 2 Corinthians, to those who or will believe, we are the fragrance of life, but to those who have chosen not to believe, we are the scent of death. Either way we possess the aroma of complete dedication. To summarize: This is how *The Lord is revealed as triumphant in your life.*

Do you have any examples of how this *aroma* in your life has affected others?_____
_____
_____
_____
_____
_____
_____

Let us take a step back for a minute. For those of you who are new to the teachings of the bible let me just clarify a couple of things. In 2 Corinthians when we are speaking of 'believing' we are talking about believing in Jesus Christ as Lord and Savior. Accepting the fact that Jesus went to the cross and died to pay for the price of your sins, because you were in no position to pay off that debt. We were also briefed on this in day 4 when we talked about the Romans 10:8-9 passage which says,

"That if you confess with your mouth, 'Jesus is Lord' and believe in your heart that God raised Him from the dead, you will be saved." Romans 10:8-9

So believing equals salvation. It means eternity in paradise with our Lord God and Father, His Son Jesus Christ, and the Holy Spirit who is here with the believers even now. In Ephesians 2:6-9 it says,

"And God raised us up with Christ and seated us with him in the heavenly realms in Christ Jesus, in order that in the coming ages He might show the incomparable riches of His grace, expressed in His kindness to us in Christ Jesus. For it is by grace you have been saved through faith—and this not from yourselves, it is the gift of God—not by works, so that no one can boast. For we are God's workmanship (works of art – paraphrase my own) created in Christ Jesus to do good works, which God prepared in advance for us to do." Ephesians 2:6-9

Today *I want you to die to the right you have to defend your name and your rights.* For Christ has already covered it with His grace.

Day 9

Father,

I confess that I know I am just flesh and blood today, and tomorrow I will be just ash and dust. May I never be so arrogant as to hold this over my adversaries. But rather use it as a means to show my equality with them and the need they too have to know about the joy of you Lord, and the salvation You so freely give. – Amen –

I don't know about you but today I feel like I have been run over by a garbage truck and then scooped up into the back and crushed again. Maybe I am just experiencing a little anxiety as to where the Oracle of Nahum is going to lead us today.

Today we will be reading Nahum 3:8-13 and focusing on **dying to our superiority over the weaker and less fortunate.** We have died to so much of ourselves. I would think this part ought to be easy. Who wants to hold on to the idea of being a bully after you have already given up almost every other area of control in your life? This brings me to a question we have not addressed yet.

Where is your identity? Have I asked you to die to that yet?   _

_____
_____
_____
_____
_____
_____

The apostle Paul writes to the church of Galatia to free the gentile converts from Old Testament rites, like circumcision. In Galatians, he teaches about the profound mystery I just questioned you on by saying,

> "I have been crucified with Christ and I no longer live, but Christ lives in me. The life I live in the body, I

live by faith in the Son of God, who loved me and gave himself for me. I do not set aside the grace of God, for if righteousness could be gained through the law, Christ died for nothing." Galatians 2:20-21

Let's go ahead and read our text over a couple of times today - Nahum 3:8-13. In verses 8-10 Nahum questions Nineveh if she is any better than Thebes, who the Assyrians just captured in 663 B.C. Nahum lists all the strengths Thebes had going for her, yet she fell to a bunch of mere soldiers. Yet we know based on Nahum 3:5-7 that Nineveh was not only going to face the forces of the Medes, Scythians, and Babylonians, but also the hand of God Almighty Himself. Looking back to the first part of Chapter 3, you can say, "Wow! God is angry."

Why is He angry?_____

_____

_____

_____

Is it because He loved Nineveh enough to forgive her and bring her back to repentance 150 years earlier?_____

_____

_____

Do you think He wanted to see the horrible 'thing' she became and the atrocities she committed?_____

_____

I feel like I have a lot of enemies at times. However, when I really search my soul it is the people closest to me that have hurt me the most. ***A voice is never raised and a weapon never drawn yet I feel paralyzed.***

Christ says,

"You have heard that it was said, 'Love your neighbor and hate your enemy.' But I tell you: Love your enemies and pray for those who persecute you, that you may be sons of your Father in heaven. He causes his sun to rise on the evil and the good, and sends rain on the righteous and the unrighteous. If you love those who love you, what reward will you get? Are not even the tax collectors doing that? And if you greet only your brothers, what are you doing more than others? Do not even pagans do that? Be perfect, therefore, as your heavenly Father is perfect." Matthew 5:43-48

What shape is your heart in? Has it been so distorted by selfishness in general that you even find it difficult to love those who love you? What efforts would have made life easier on your loved one? What efforts have you missed?_____
_____
_____
_____

I let my wife down tonight. Lord please, forgive me. Help me to be stronger in my weakness and rely more upon you so my heart cries out to you O Lord and you alone for strength.
– Amen –

Have you ever felt that way with your spouse or loved ones?   _
_____
_____

What are we doing more than others to love our enemies?   _
_____
_____
_____

In order to love our enemies, we are going to need to reshape our hearts to

"Be perfect, therefore as your heavenly Father is perfect." Matthew 5:48

Christ is our ideal example on the cross as He died for our sins. Are you ready to die for your enemy?_____

_____

Moving along as we visit verses 11-13, we find Nineveh getting drunk. The fortress was invaded and the armies looted the wealth; like figs falling off the tree into the open mouths of the first eaters. Finally, the gates are damaged beyond repair and just waiting for the enemy to invade. Do you think it was because they were drunk on God's wrath?_____

_____

_____

Are you ready to reshape your heart for the inferior and less fortunate?

Day 10

Dear Lord,

We have gone through so much on this short journey. But ultimately Lord, we ask that You help us to die to everything that hinders our relationship with You, so that we may truly live the life You have purposed for us. – Amen –

Please read Nahum 3:14-19 a couple times over.

Nineveh's end has come; just as Nahum prophesized in 1:8 He (God) pursued her into darkness. In the finale, it did not make a difference how she strengthened her defenses. She was just consumed. Even with the oracle of warning, Nineveh did not seem prepared for the destruction that would completely consume her for eternity. It was not even until 1845 A.D. that archeologists finally unburied her ruins. Centuries passed and silence consumed her.

What is your response to this? Do you find this just and fair? _

_____
_____
_____
_____

How does this make you feel about allowing sin to continue to take hold of your life?_____
_____
_____
_____

My whole objective of this devotional bible study has been for you to *die to everything that hinders your relationship with God.* So that you may live, and may live life in its complete fullness (that you may be perfect in the sight of God through the cleansing sacrifice made by His One and Only Perfect Son, Jesus Christ our Lord and Savior).

Remember everyone; this is an ongoing journey that does not end until you look our Lord Jesus face to face in the eyes. So please revisit this - challenge yourself again, and with parts of your life you never even realized existed before.

I don't know about you but I have found towards the end of this bible study that I have experienced many trials and tribulations.

"...I will bring them into the fire; I will refine them like silver and test them like gold. They will call on my name and I will answer them; I will say, 'They are my people,' and they will say, 'The Lord is our God.'" Zechariah 13:9

Of course this quote is taken from Zechariah when Israel comes to recognize Jesus as their Messianic King. Still that is how I feel like I am being refined some days. – Amen –

This message in James has been so comforting to me which says,

"Consider it pure joy, my brothers, whenever you face trials of many kinds, because you know that the testing of your faith develops perseverance. Perseverance must finish its work so that you may be mature and complete, not lacking anything. If any of you lack wisdom, he should ask God, who gives generously to all without finding fault, and it will be given to him. But when he asks, he must believe and not doubt, because he who doubts is like a wave of the sea, blown and tossed by the wind. That man should not think he will receive anything from the Lord; he is a double-minded man, unstable in all he does." James 1:2-8

This passage is so reassuring because I am reminded that "Perseverance must finish its work so that you may be mature and *complete*, not lacking anything." James 1:4

If you have never made a complete commitment to the Lord, or may be wondering where you stand with the Lord right now, just go back and review days 4 & 8. They give you a clear picture of how to release your life into the loving hands of our Lord, God and Savior. John 3:16 says,

"For God so loved the world that he gave his one and only Son, that whoever believes in him shall not perish but have eternal life." John 3:16

If you are desiring eternal life now, get on your knees, confess your sins, acknowledge you need Jesus' help, and state you are ready to follow Jesus the King above all Kings to wherever He may call you. He has an important plan for you that only you can fulfill.

Do you feel changed, have you died to everything we have spoken about over these past 10 days of study?

I want you to take a moment and go look in the mirror. What do you notice: any changes, any differences? Write what you see with as much detail as you desire._____

_____
_____
_____
_____
_____
_____
_____

Turn the page

I want you to take notice what you saw in that mirror. It is the raw material of what kings and queens are made of!

For you died to all parts of yourself and can proudly say,

"But if Christ is in you, your body is dead because of sin, yet your spirit is alive because of righteousness. And if the Spirit of him who raised Jesus from the dead is living in you, he who raised Christ from the dead will also give live to your mortal bodies through his Spirit, who lives in you." Romans 8:10-11

List of things we are dying to:

Day 1 Die to the control you think you have on your life.

What control issue did you feel you had to die to in your life? _
_____
_____
_____

Day 2 Die to the picture perfect life you have always dreamt of.

What part of your picture perfect life do you need to let go of? _
_____
_____
_____

Day 3 Die to a life of self-indulgence.

Where do you feel you could spend a little less time and money?_____
_____
_____

Day 4 Die to your own plans of travel/vacation and destination.

Is there a place in your life that has a grip on you that you just need to release?_____
_____
_____

Day 5 Die to the idea of being held captive by life's circumstances.

What has kept you from joining Jesus at the table?_____
_____
_____
_____

Day 6   Die to the idea that there is never a new day.

What does a new day look like for you?_____
_____
_____
_____

Day 7   Die to the security you hold in your social standings, employment status, and entitlements.

If you're just a nobody what would you be free to do?_____
_____
_____
_____

Day 8   Die to the right to defend your name, and your rights.

Who would you be if you had to be someone else?_____
_____
_____
_____

Day 9   Die to your superiority over the weak and less fortunate.

What keeps you from making friends with the janitor?_____
_____
_____
_____

Day 10 Die to everything that hinders your relationship with Father God.

What is stopping you?_____
_____
_____
_____

EPILOGUE

Following 10 Days to Die, I am planning on releasing two more devotional studies to complete the series in 2013. I have not decided on a title for the second piece of work yet. However, it will be something close to 10 Days to rejuvenation, relaxation or rest. The final book in the series will be titled '10 Days to Armor Up' and you should expect to see this in the fall of 2013. It will cover conquering life's battles on a daily basis.

Hope you enjoy the entire series as much as I will, in creating them under the guidance of the Holy Spirit. I hope you all may be blessed beyond belief!

ACKNOWLEDGMENTS

To Sarah, and Davita Gingras, for all the times I missed you while I was working on this manuscript.

To Sharmini Gingras, for all your persistent encouragement and love while I worked on this project and the patience exercised in editing my work.

To Dr. Larry Vold, for your relentless love for God and all the blessings I received listening to you preach His word.

To Dr. Bill Temple, for all your kind words and encouragement.

To My Parents Ron, and Jan Williams for just being there.

To Heather Thurston, for helping pull the final project together with your editing skills.

REFERENCES

J. HamptomKeathley IV, Th.M.. Nahum

http://www.bible.org/docs/ot/books/minorp/nahum.htm

John Gill, Exposition of Nahum, e-Sword®, Version 7.1.0

The NIV Study Bible Copyright© 1985 by The Zondervan Corporation

Henry T. Blackaby& Claude V. King. Experiencing God, Knowing and Doing the Will of God, LifeWay Press (1990)

www.ingramcontent.com/pod-product-compliance
Lightning Source LLC
Chambersburg PA
CBHW060619030426

42337CB00018B/3122